The information provided in this book is intended for general informational purposes only. Please be aware that the field of artificial intelligence is a rapidly evolving domain with ongoing advancements and changes.

While efforts have been made to ensure the accuracy and reliability of the information presented, the author cannot guarantee its comprehensiveness or timeliness. Therefore, readers should exercise discretion and seek up-to-date resources and expert advice for specific matters.

The author and publisher disclaim any liability for any loss, damage, or inconvenience caused as a result of the use or reliance on the information provided in this book. Readers are encouraged to independently verify information and make their own informed decisions.

Please note that the examples and suggestions provided are for illustrative purposes and should not be considered as endorsements or guarantees.

Thank you for your understanding and for being a part of this dynamic journey.

COPYRIGHT

All rights reserved. No part of this publication may be reproduced, distributed, or transmitted in any form or by any means, including photocopying, recording, or any other electronic or mechanical methods, without the prior written permission of the author. Unauthorized use, reproduction, or transmission of any portion of this publication may result in severe civil and criminal penalties under applicable copyright laws.

The information and content contained in this book are protected by copyright laws and are provided for general informational purposes only. While every effort has been made to ensure the accuracy and reliability of the information presented, the author assumes no responsibility or liability for any errors, omissions, or damages arising from the use of the information contained within this publication.

Thank you for respecting the intellectual property rights and understanding the terms of this copyright notice. Your compliance with these guidelines is greatly appreciated.

TABLE OF CONTENT

SR NO.	TITLE	PAGE NO.
1	Introduction	1
2	What the Heck is ChatGPT and How Does It Differ From Google?	4
3	Getting Started with CHATGPT	12
4	Tips on How to Utilize CHATGPT Effectively	15
5	Magically 100x Your Productivity	22
6	Social Media Marketing	52
7	Monetizing with ChatGPT	72
8	Make it big with Freelancing	107
9	Limitations	116

INTRODUCTION

In the heart of the evolution of technology is a revolution that is shaking up the way people and computers work together and changing the way we live, work, and even think. Welcome to the age of artificial intelligence (AI), where software and systems can imitate human intelligence by learning from experiences, adapting to new information, and doing tasks that used to require human intelligence.

AI has led to the creation of many new tools and apps that can be used in a wide range of industries, jobs, and hobbies. AI is becoming an important part of our everyday lives. It is used to predict weather, patterns and save energy, power virtual personal assistants, and make games that are very immersive. It's no longer just about replacing people in jobs that require a lot of physical labor; it's also about giving us new ways to be creative, get more done, and even enjoy our free time.

Now, among these powerful AI apps, there is one platform called ChatGPT that has shot to fame and made a name for itself as the tech platform that has grown the fastest in history. In fact, it reached the amazing milestone of 100 million users faster than any other platform before it. In just five days, it had a million users. It's a fantastic thing to accomplish, isn't it? The best part is that the magic has only just begun. Who knows what new and amazing things ChatGPT might have already done by the time you read this?

We shall soon understand what is ChatGPT, and how can it change the way you do things? ChatGPT has a lot of potential, whether you're an entrepreneur, a student, a teacher, a writer, a coder, or just someone who wants to find new ways to improve their everyday life.

Now do you often find yourself procrastinating over tasks that require critical thinking? Does the thought of crafting a professional email fill you with dread? Does your mind go blank when you have to write a blog post or a story that people will want to read? Or maybe you want to make your own online course but don't know where to begin.

Well, don't worry, because ChatGPT is here.

In upcoming chapters, we'll talk about how ChatGPT can change these and many other parts of your life. Imagine having a virtual assistant that not only makes you more productive but also helps you tap into your creativity and take it to new heights. That's how ChatGPT works.

So, are you ready to join us on this exciting journey to find out more about ChatGPT and how to use it to your advantage at work and in life? Let's dive in!

From now on, we will frequently mention the term "prompt." A prompt is like an instruction or topic that you provide to guide an AI model, such as ChatGPT. It helps the AI generate a response or continue the conversation in a specific direction. Think of it as a starting point for the AI. Just like people use search terms on Google, with ChatGPT, we use prompts to guide its responses. By using effective prompts, you can receive better and more relevant responses from the AI model.

CHAPTER 1 : What the Heck is ChatGPT and How Does It Differ From Google?

At its core, ChatGPT is an advanced language model developed by OpenAI. Google is a search engine that pulls information from the internet. ChatGPT, on the other hand, makes new content based on the information it was taught. Google is like a librarian who gives you books (web pages) based on what you want.

ChatGPT, on the other hand, is more like a skilled writer who can make a unique story (a response) based on what you tell it or what you ask it to do.

Let's look at an example to see what I mean.

If I search for something on Google,
EXAMPLE:

"LIST OF FIRST 15 PRESIDENTS OF THE UNITED STATES WITH THEIR BIRTHDATE"

Let's look at an example to see what I mean.

This is what I get as an answer :

Google   LIST OF FIRST 15 PRESIDENTS OF THE UNI   ✕

Q All   □ Images   🗐 News   📕 Books   ⊘ Shopping   ⋮ More

About 10,30,00,000 results (0.54 seconds)

Library of Congress (.gov)
https://www.loc.gov › print › list › 057_chron

Chronological List of Presidents, First Ladies, and Vice ...

YEAR	PRESIDENT	VICE PRESIDENT
1789-1797	George Washington	John Adams
1797-1801	John Adams	Thomas Jefferson
1801-1805	Thomas Jefferson	Aaron Burr

Now lets try the same on CHATGPT

Here is a list of the first 15 Presidents of the United States along with their birthdates:

1. George Washington: February 22, 1732
2. John Adams: October 30, 1735
3. Thomas Jefferson: April 13, 1743
4. James Madison: March 16, 1751
5. James Monroe: April 28, 1758
6. John Quincy Adams: July 11, 1767
7. Andrew Jackson: March 15, 1767
8. Martin Van Buren: December 5, 1782
9. William Henry Harrison: February 9, 1773
10. John Tyler: March 29, 1790
11. James K. Polk: November 2, 1795
12. Zachary Taylor: November 24, 1784
13. Millard Fillmore: January 7, 1800
14. Franklin Pierce: November 23, 1804
15. James Buchanan: April 23, 1791

Do you see the difference?

CHATGPT understands the prompt as if it were speaking to you and provides you with a list of the things we asked for.

Though, that's just the beginning.

Say you want to write a passive-aggressive email to a company that won't give you your money back. You are their regular customer so you dont even want to be harsh but at the same time sound firm.

PROMPT : "Write a passive-aggressive email to the ABC company, with whom I frequently travel, requesting a refund for a trip that I did not take."

CHATGPT RESPONSE :

Subject: Refund Request: Unattended Trip

Dear ABC Company,
I am writing to address an issue regarding a recent trip that I did not take. It seems there has been a mistake in your records, leading to the false

assumption that I went on this particular journey.
When I received the bill for the trip, I was surprised to see charges for an experience I never had. As a loyal customer who often travels with ABC Company, I trust that you will promptly look into this matter and provide a refund for the trip I did not attend.

I kindly request your investigation into this mix-up and a quick resolution to ensure such misunderstandings are avoided in the future. Thank you for your attention, and I look forward to hearing from you soon.

Sincerely,
[Your Name]

Impressed? Well there is a lot more that we could do.

Let's think of four words at random and turn them into a poem.

THE FIRST ONES THAT COME TO MIND ARE " apple , alien , shoes , football"

PROMPT : "Using these words to make a fantastic poem "apple , alien , shoes , football"

CHATGPT RESPONSE :

In a realm where imagination thrives,
An apple, an alien, shoes, and football collide.
A crimson apple, crisp and sweet,
An alien, enigmatic and discreet.
Shoes, a humble companion to our feet,
And football, a sport where passion meets.
The apple symbolizes knowledge's quest,
While the alien sparks curiosity, zest.

Shoes carry us through life's winding ways,
And football unites, in joyous displays.
Together, they weave a tapestry unique,
Where diverse elements harmoniously speak.
A fusion of flavors, unknown and grand,
The apple, alien, shoes, and football hand in hand.
In this whimsical world, their stories unfold,
A testament to unity, in tales untold.

CHATGPT wrote this in 2 second, to test it yourself

provide ChatGPT any word and ask it to make a poem , write a story , make a plot or anything and it will do that in a matter of minutes, we will get in into details later ahead.

Imagine you're reading a book and you come across a line so confusing that you have to call a doctor friend to find out what it means.

"The patient has experienced an acute myocardial infarction, exacerbated by underlying comorbidities including hypertension and hyperlipidemia."

In a matter of seconds CHATGPT can write this in a simple language, you just have to ask it.

PROMPT :
"The patient has experienced an acute myocardial infarction, exacerbated by underlying comorbidities including hypertension and hyperlipidemia, explain this in a simple language"

ChatGPT RESPONSE : "The patient has had a heart attack, which was made worse by other health problems they have, including high blood pressure and high cholesterol."

Well CHATGPT can do pretty much anything, you can ask it to make a complicated sentence simple or a simple sentence complicated , its a master of words.

GENERATING STORY IDEAS

Suppose you're an aspiring writer and you're struggling with writer's block. You can give ChatGPT the simplest of **PROMPT *like :"a cat in a magical forest"***, and it could provide you with a captivating story idea:
EG :

CHATGPT RESPONSE :
In a magical forest full of sparkling light, there was a special cat. This cat had a unique ability to talk to the mystical creatures living there. The cat acted as a protector and had the important task of bringing balance back to the forest whenever its magical powers were in danger.

ASSISTING WITH LANGUAGE LEARNING

If you're learning a new language and are stuck understanding a difficult sentence, ChatGPT can help. For example, you might input a complex Spanish sentence and ChatGPT could provide a translation, and also explain any difficult grammatical constructs present in the sentence.

CRAFTING UNIQUE RECIPES

Wondering what to cook for dinner? No worries! ChatGPT can assist you with that. Simply provide a list of ingredients you have, and it can come up with a recipe for you. For instance, if you mention having chicken, broccoli, cheese, and pasta, ChatGPT might suggest a delicious option like a creamy chicken and broccoli pasta bake. It can even provide you with a variety of unique recipes to choose from.

CHAPTER 2 : GETTING STARTED WITH CHATGPT

Simply go to CHAT.OPENAI.COM and sign up

These are 2 models of CHATGPT that you will see as soon as you sign up

GPT3.5 is the free model and GPT 4 is only available to paid users for $20 a month.

If you are starting out, you can simply start with GPT3.5 as it pretty much gets any job done.
GPT 4 has an added advantage which is it has access to browsing feature.

Which means if you get a paid model . GPT 4 can search the web and bring you results as CHATGPT was only trained on data until September 2021.

This can be a game changer for many people

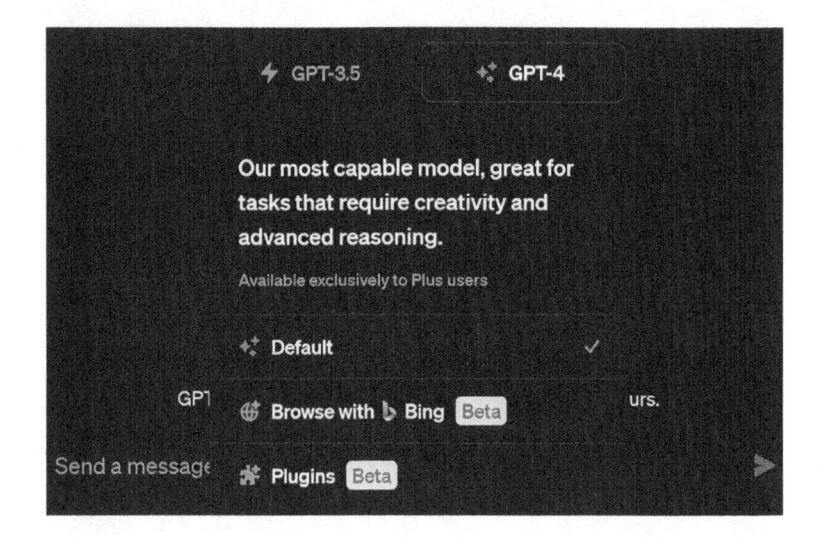

Once you pay for GPT 4 you'll have access to Default responses by ChatGPT, along with a switch button that allows you to directly explore the web. By using GPT-4, you'll receive real-time responses based on the prompt you provide. This enables you to access a wide range of information and get immediate answers from the AI model.

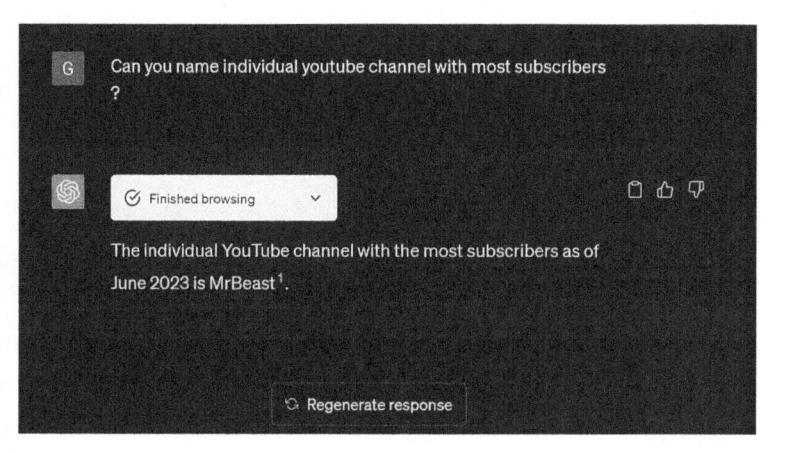

> G: Can you name individual youtube channel with most subscribers?
>
> ⓖ ✓ Finished browsing
>
> The individual YouTube channel with the most subscribers as of June 2023 is MrBeast[1].

If we asked the same question to GPT 3.5 it would not have the answer to this question.

Since GPT 4 has access to real time data , it was able to pull the information and provide us with the exact answer.

It should be noted that the real-time browsing capabilities of GPT-4 are presently in the beta phase. While the efficiency of its query searches may currently vary, we anticipate substantial improvements aligned with advancements in artificial intelligence. As technology continues to evolve, we can expect significant enhancements in GPT-4's real-time browsing capabilities, further augmenting its overall functionality.

CHAPTER 3 :Tips on How to Utilize CHATGPT Effectively

CHATGPT is a powerful tool that can assist users in various ways. However, it's important to understand its limitations to maximize its potential. Often it can get a little tricky initially as how how CHATGPT will respond to you.

To maximize the effectiveness of ChatGPT in generating the desired output, precision is key. For instance, if you wish to write an essay on the topic of "Global Warming," providing an open-ended prompt might result in lengthy or less focused responses. A more effective approach is to be specific and provide clear instructions.

For example:

PROMPT: *"Write an essay on Global Warming in under 250 words, focusing on the latest developments primarily."*

By providing a precise prompt, including word limit and specific focus areas, you can guide ChatGPT to generate a more concise and relevant essay tailored to your requirements.

CHATGPT Response :

"Introduction: Global warming, a pressing environmental issue, continues to escalate with devastating consequences for our planet. In recent years, the world has witnessed significant developments related to this crisis, highlighting the urgency of taking immediate action…"

Well obviously chatgpt wrote a big answer and I cut it out but I am sure you understood how it works.

If we just asked chatgpt to write on global warming it would have gone on and on probably talking about things that we might not need now.

Another example could be you, lets say you want to visit rome under 6 hours walking , we would have to say something like :

PROMPT : "I want to visit rome , Ill start walking around 4pm and Ill walk until its 10pm, tell me exactly how I can plan my day"

CHATGPT RESPONSE :

"Start at the Colosseum.
Visit the Roman Forum and Capitoline Hill.
Proceed to the Trevi Fountain.
Explore the Spanish Steps.
Continue to Piazza Navona.
Conclude your day at the Pantheon"

Keep in mind that you can always ask CHATGPT to be more specific, and it will tell you when you can start and how long it will take to get from one place to another.

Now if you want to know what can be done after 10pm with a friend of yours , You can type something like ,

Prompt : "What to do in rome after 10pm, I would like to have a beer in some silent place with a buddy of mine, give me a list of 5 such places"

CHATGPT RESPONSE :
" Ma Che Siete Venuti a Fà (Trastevere)
Birreria Trilussa (Trastevere)

Open Baladin Roma
Birra del Borgo (Piazza Trilussa)
Freni e Frizioni (Trastevere)"

The point here is to play around with CHATGPT and get to a point where it does what you want, you will have to play with it a little and find that sweet spot where it does what you want without overdoing it.

One interesting thing about ChatGPT is that you can tell it to mimic the speech or style of a certain person.

PROMPT : "I have had a good time in rome, now I am in venice, tell me what I can do in venice from 12pm to 9pm, write it in 8 sentences and write in the style of popular rapper EMINEM"

CHATGPT RESPONSE :

"From noon to nine, Venice is the place to be,
Start at Piazza San Marco, soak in the history.
Gondola ride through canals, Rialto Bridge's glory,
Doge's Palace, majestic rooms, telling tales of old stories.

Get lost in the streets, discover hidden treasures,
End with a sunset at Grand Canal, memories to measure.
Venice, a city of romance, where dreams come true,
In those nine hours, embrace its magic, enjoy the view".

Well that's interesting and incase you didn't like the poem, chat gpt can do it millions of times, just press on "REGENRATE RESPONSE" and magically you now have a new poem.

One important thing for you to remember is to not settle at the initial response . CHATGPT CAN DO IT MILLIONS of times so why not try 10 times until you are fully satisfied by the response.

Now lets say you ask CHATGPT to write a blog post under 500 words and you do not like it, you can ask it to do again and again.

You can ask it for something like

PROMPT "I want to write a blog post on iPhone and Apple company, make sure you talk about :

Who started the company , Major stakeholders , When did the market capitalization of Apple hit a trillion dollar first time"

Now that you have added these 3 points , CHATGPT will alter itself to your needs and create the post according , here is the example. I asked it to do under 150 words, so you get an idea.

CHATGPT RESPONSE : "Apple, founded by Steve Jobs, Steve Wozniak, and Ronald Wayne in 1976, is a renowned technology company that has revolutionized the industry. With Steve Jobs at the helm, Apple introduced groundbreaking products such as the Macintosh, iPod, iPhone, and iPad, which propelled the company to new heights.

Major stakeholders in Apple include its co-founder Steve Wozniak, CEO Tim Cook, and a diverse group of institutional and individual shareholders. The company has built a loyal customer base and has consistently ranked among the most valuable brands globally.

In August 2018, Apple achieved a historic milestone when its market capitalization hit a trillion dollars for the first time. This remarkable achievement was driven by the success of its flagship products, strategic acquisitions, and its ecosystem of services. It solidified Apple's position as one of the most valuable companies in the world, showcasing its impact and dominance in the technology industry."

Do not forget that CHATGPT can often get it wrong and needs a human revision at the end. It is powerful but not perfect. It may occasionally generate incorrect information.

CHAPTER 4: MAGICALLY 100X YOUR PRODUCTIVITY

Ah, the pleasure of getting things done! We've all been in situations where we had a lot to do and wished we had more help to deal with life's problems. But don't worry, my fellow friends! In this amazing age of technology, we have a special genie at our hands who can help us in the most useful and funny ways.

Why rely on other people or hire someone else to do your work when CHATGPT is here and can wave its virtual wand? It's like having a personal helper, a wise mentor, and a huge library all in one. And what's best? It's free of charge! Well, unless you choose to be a paid member. Hey, even magical genies have to pay to keep the lights on, right?

Just think about how many problems, big and small, would go away if you could just click your keys. Whether you're a teacher trying to inspire young minds, a student looking for a way out before a test, a business owner navigating the tough world of business, or even a lawyer trying to figure out the complicated world of law, don't worry! AI is here to help you out and make your life much easier.

It's like having a good friend who can play any part you want. Need help grading a mountain of papers? They will only take CHATGPT a few minutes to go through. Having trouble with a hard math problem? See how it comes up with answers faster than you can say "abracadabra." Researching the law got you in a bind? With a digital twist, CHATGPT will solve the riddles of case law like Sherlock Holmes.

And let's not forget that this great helper is also a lot of fun. CHATGPT can make you laugh with jokes, tell you stories about strange worlds, and talk to you in a way that will make you smile. Who said being useful had to be boring? CHATGPT will help you get ahead by making you laugh.

This chapter is going to get you all started. I am going to show you exactly what I would type in and what CHATGPT would do.

BLOG POSTS

Before we begin, I'm sure you're already familiar with what a blog post is. However, let me explain it in simple terms once again for clarity.

"A blog post is a piece of writing that you create and publish on the internet for others to read. It's like writing a story or an article that you want to share with people. It can be about anything you're passionate about, whether it's your favorite hobbies, your travels, or even your creative ideas. Blog posts can include text, images, and sometimes even videos, making them exciting and engaging for readers of all ages."

But the tricky part is creating a blog posts can require enormous hard work and ming boggling research, you would have to :

1 : Choose a topic that is backed by reputable sources to ensure the accuracy of your information.

2 Craft an attention-grabbing title that sparks curiosity and entices readers to dive into your blog post.

3 Structure your blog post with clear organization, including paragraphs, sections, and headings, to enhance readability.

4 Engage your audience by incorporating storytelling, personal experiences, or thought-provoking questions to make your content captivating.

5 Before hitting that publish button, meticulously proofread and edit your blog post, paying close attention to grammar, typos, and overall clarity.

6 : Consider SEO (Search Engine Optimization) techniques to improve the visibility and reach of your blog post. Incorporate relevant keywords naturally throughout your content, optimize headings and meta descriptions, and ensure your post is mobile-friendly to enhance its search engine ranking and attract more organic traffic

BUT, all this was until CHATGPT existed.
 Now you are just a few clicks away and boom.

Lets say you are interested in writing a blog post about : " Weight loss " .

I am just using the easiest example to start with then we can go ahead.

We can simply start by saying

PROMPT: Write a blog post on weight loss for men over the age of 50 "

CHATGPT Response : "Introduction: Maintaining a healthy weight becomes increasingly important as we age, especially for men over 50. However, shedding those extra pounds might feel like an uphill battle. Fear not! In this blog post, we will explore practical and effective weight loss tips tailored specifically for men in this age group. Let's embark on a journey towards improved health, increased vitality, and a more confident version of yourself!

1. Prioritize a Balanced Diet: A nutritious and well-balanced diet is the foundation of successful weight loss. Opt for whole, unprocessed foods rich in fiber, lean proteins, fruits, vegetables, and healthy fats. Incorporate portion control to manage calorie intake and avoid excessive snacking. Remember, consistency is key!

2 : Stay Hydrated: Hydration is often overlooked but plays a vital role in weight loss. Drinking enough water throughout the day helps curb appetite, boosts metabolism, and supports overall health. Aim for at least 8 cups (64 ounces) of water daily, and limit sugary beverages that can contribute to weight gain."

Well the actually post is really big, I have just added the initial part so you know how it works.

A better way would be to ask CHATGPT to create an outline and then we can structure our blog in a better way.

PROMPT : "Create an outline for a blog post about weight loss for men over the age of 50 focusing mainly on exercise"

CHATGPT RESPONSE
:
I. Introduction
A. Importance of exercise for weight loss in men over 50
B. Setting realistic goals and expectations

II. Understanding the Benefits of Exercise
A. Boosting metabolism and calorie burn

B. Preserving muscle mass and bone density

C. Enhancing cardiovascular health and reducing the risk of chronic diseases

III. Types of Exercises for Weight Loss

A. Cardiovascular Exercises

1. Brisk walking or jogging

2. Cycling or stationary biking

3. Swimming or water aerobics

B. Strength Training Exercises

1. Resistance training with weights or resistance bands

2. Bodyweight exercises (push-ups, squats, lunges, etc.)

3. Functional training for overall strength and balance

Again, I cut it down, but here's how it works: You can easily add more points to this plan, reorganize it, ask CHATGPT to make more points, and so on.

Now lets say you want to write something on weight loss but you have no clue what. Again we can do something like

PROMPT : "GIVE ME 5 TITLE IDEAS FOR TO WRITE A BLOG ON WEIGHT LOSS, CHOOSE THE NICHE WITH LOWEST COMPETITION"

CHATGPT RESPONSE :

"Certainly! Here are five title ideas for a blog on weight loss, focusing on a niche with lower competition:

1. "Gentle and Effective: A Guide to Weight Loss for Men Over 50"
2. "Effortless Weight Loss: Simple Strategies for Busy Moms"
3. "Weight Loss for Beginners: Your Step-by-Step Journey to a Healthier You"
4. "Breaking Barriers: Unlocking Sustainable Weight Loss for Office Workers"
5. "Empowering Weight Loss: Mindful Eating for Emotional Wellness"

Now, you can ask CHATGPT to elaborate on any points or just regenerate an answer if you'd like.

In conclusion, CHATGPT can be used to create outstanding blog posts.

COLD OUTREACH EMAIL :

We've all faced that daunting task of composing the perfect email, struggling to find the right words, tone, and structure. Whether it's a cold outreach email or a blog post, the pressure to deliver a compelling message can be overwhelming. But fear not! Thanks to the incredible capabilities of ChatGPT, crafting impeccable emails.

Normally you'd have to spend hours for :
1:Choosing an attention-grabbing subject line: Spark curiosity and entice the recipient to open your email by crafting a subject line that stands out.

2:Personalize the email: Demonstrate genuine interest and show that you've done your research. Mention specific details or recent accomplishments of the recipient to create a connection.

3:Clearly state your purpose: Be concise and upfront about why you're reaching out. State your intentions and what you hope to achieve with the email.

4:Craft a well-structured message: Organize your

email into paragraphs or sections to enhance readability. Use clear and concise language to convey your message effectively.

5:Engage the recipient: Incorporate storytelling, personal experiences, or thought-provoking questions to make your email captivating and foster a connection with the reader.

6:Meticulously proofread and edit: Pay close attention to grammar, spelling, and overall clarity. Ensure that your email is error-free and presents you in the best possible light.

7:End with a clear call to action: Wrap up your email by stating what you would like the recipient to do next. Whether it's scheduling a meeting, providing feedback, or taking any specific action, make it easy for them to respond.

But now you are just a click away.
Lets say you are lawyer wanting to intern at a reputable law firm, you'd write.

PROMPT : "Write a cold outreach email which

would help me intern at most reputable firms in New York"

CHATGPT RESPONSE :

Subject: Enthusiastic Law Student Seeking Internship Opportunity at Prestigious New York Firms

Dear [Hiring Manager's Name],

I am writing to express my deep interest in securing an internship opportunity at a prestigious law firm in New York. As a dedicated law student with a passion for excellence, I am eager to contribute to [Firm's Name] and gain valuable insights into the legal profession.

With a strong academic background in law and a solid foundation in key legal concepts, I am equipped with the analytical and research skills necessary to excel in an internship role. Additionally, my involvement in [relevant extracurricular activities] has honed my ability to think critically and work effectively in a team-oriented environment.

I am particularly drawn to [Firm's Name] for its renowned reputation, commitment to client service, and cutting-edge legal work. I am confident that my enthusiasm, dedication, and strong work ethic would make me a valuable asset to your firm.

Attached is my resume for your review. I would appreciate the opportunity to discuss potential internship openings and further demonstrate how my skills and experiences align with the needs of [Firm's Name]. Thank you for considering my application.

I look forward to the possibility of contributing to [Firm's Name] as an intern and gaining invaluable professional experience. Please feel free to contact me at [your email address] or [your phone number] if you require any additional information.

Thank you for your time and consideration.

Sincerely,
[Your Name]

Though you must know it is not perfect , you will need to play around a bit to again find that point where CHATGPT does what you really want it to do or lets say You are a sales representative reaching out to a potential client through a cold outreach email.

PROMPT : Write a email introducing your product or service, highlighting its unique features and benefits, and expressing your interest in exploring potential collaboration with the recipient."

CHATGPT RESPONSE :

Subject: Introducing [Product/Service]: Enhance Your Business's Success

Dear [Recipient's Name],

I hope this email finds you well. My name is [Your Name], and I am a dedicated sales representative at [Your Company]. I am reaching out to introduce our innovative [Product/Service] and explore the opportunity for collaboration with your esteemed organization.

At [Your Company], we understand the challenges businesses face in today's competitive landscape. That's why we have developed [Product/Service], a cutting-edge solution designed to help businesses like yours achieve unparalleled success.

[Product/Service] offers a range of unique features that set it apart from the competition. From [highlight key feature #1], providing streamlined and efficient workflows, to [highlight key feature #2], enhancing productivity and driving growth, our solution is tailored to meet your specific needs.

By leveraging [Product/Service], your business can experience significant boost in [specific benefits]

such as increased operational efficiency, cost savings, and improved customer satisfaction. Our solution has been proven to deliver tangible results for businesses across various industries, as demonstrated by our satisfied clientele.

I would love the opportunity to discuss how [Product/Service] can address your business's unique requirements and contribute to your success. I am confident that our solution aligns perfectly with your goals and vision.

Please let me know a convenient time for a call or meeting, and I will gladly provide a more in-depth overview of [Product/Service]. I look forward to the possibility of collaborating with your esteemed organization and helping you achieve new heights of success.

Thank you for considering our offering, and I remain at your disposal for any further information or questions you may have.

Best regards,

[Your Name] [Your Title/Position] [Your Company]

Again you can simple set the tone as well, if case you didn't like the response.

You can simple play around saying .

PROMPT : Rewrite the email as if you were DONALD TRUMP

CHATGPT RESPONSE:
Subject: Tremendous Opportunity Awaits - Let's Make Business Great Again!

Dear [Recipient's Name],

I hope you're doing fantastic, absolutely fantastic. It's Donald J. Trump, the very successful and incredible businessman reaching out to you with an offer you can't resist. Believe me, this is going to be huge!

I'm thrilled to introduce you to our amazing product/service, [Product/Service]. Let me tell you, it's tremendous. It's the best, folks. No one does it better than us. [Product/Service] is a game-changer that will revolutionize your business. It's a winner!

With [Product/Service], you'll experience unmatched features that will skyrocket your success. We're talking about incredible efficiency with [highlight key feature #1] and mind-blowing results through [highlight key feature #2]. It's a winning combination that guarantees tremendous results for your business.

I've seen firsthand how [Product/Service] has transformed countless businesses. It's truly incredible. Just imagine the possibilities! You'll witness soaring productivity, significant cost savings, and customers will love you. They really will. You'll be winning like never before.

I'm excited to discuss this opportunity with you, to make your business great again. Together, we'll conquer the competition and achieve tremendous success. Let's schedule a call or meeting at your convenience. Believe me, it will be the best decision you've ever made.

Thank you for considering this fantastic offer. I'm here to answer any questions you may have and provide more details. Let's get started on this incredible journey to make your business the greatest it can be.

Looking forward to speaking with you soon.

Best regards,
Donald J. Trump

SKYROCKET YOUR TWITTER SUCCESS WITH CHATGPT: UNLEASH VIRAL TWEETING POWER

Twitter, the popular social media platform known for its concise and real-time conversations, has become a go-to platform for individuals and businesses to connect with a large audience. In this fast-paced digital world, gaining attention on Twitter is crucial. One effective strategy to achieve this is by creating viral-style tweets using ChatGPT.

How often do you see some with a tweet like this

"1   The secret to weight loss: Nourish your body with nutritious foods and watch the pounds melt away. Let's eat smart and slim down! #WeightLossSecrets #HealthyLiving"

2. "   Get moving, shed those pounds! Exercise is the ultimate secret weapon for weight loss success. Let's sweat it out and achieve our fitness goals! ♀ #FitnessMotivation #WeightLossGoals"

3. "   Unlock the power of mindset: Believe in yourself, set achievable goals, and embrace self-

compassion. Let's change our mindset and watch the pounds disappear! #WeightLossMindset #PositiveChange"

and wonder who on earth has so that much time to add perfect emoticons , use perfect hashtags and at the same time also make it sound perfectly catchy?

Well, CHATGPT is here.

One might use viral-style tweets to advertise their business on TWITTER or just write interesting tweets to get followers, like

Let's imagine you run a DONUT business and are building your first store in Ohio.

You could simply go like

PROMPT : I have a new donut store opening up in Ohio , create a viral and catchy tweet for twitter so people know about my new store

CHATGPT RESPONSE :

" Need a donut-related pick-me-up? Here's a sweet joke to brighten your day: Why did the donut go to the dentist? Because it needed a chocolate filling extraction! 😁 Now that we've got your smile going, get ready to have your taste buds smiling too with the grand opening of [Your Donut Store Name] in Ohio! Get ready for donut-filled bliss and laughter that's glazed and amused.   #DonutHumor #SweetLaughs"

We can write it in Eminem Style

PROMPT : " I have a new donut store opening up in Ohio , create a viral and catchy tweet for twitter so people know about my new store, write the tweet in Eminem style "

CHATGPT RESPONSE : "   Yo, listen up, donut lovers! We're droppin' bars sweeter than sugar, hotter than a fryer. [Your Donut Store Name] in Ohio is the real deal, bringin' the flavor that'll make you squeal. From the classics to mind-blowin' creations, our donuts are straight-up lyrical sensations. Get ready to devour, no holdin' back, 'cause we're takin' donuts to a whole new track! #DonutFlow #SweetRhymes"

You could also ask CHATGPT to review a book in 5 tweets and you can pick any niche and start tweeting about it regularly and engage with others which will help you pick up fast. We could start like ***PROMPT :5 LESSIONS LEARN FROM BOOK RICH DAD , POOR DAD" Create a thread of 5 tweets***

CHATGPT RESPONSE :

1/5: Financial education is crucial for success. "Rich Dad, Poor Dad" teaches the importance of understanding money, investing, and building assets. #FinancialEducation

2/5: Focus on income-generating assets, not liabilities. Acquire assets that put money in your pocket and avoid liabilities that drain your finances. #AssetsOverLiabilities

3/5: Develop an abundance mindset and embrace opportunities. Think like an entrepreneur, identify possibilities, and take calculated risks. #AbundanceMindset #Entrepreneurship

4/5: Break free from the rat race. Strive for financial independence, where passive income exceeds expenses. Escape the cycle of living paycheck to paycheck. #FinancialIndependence

5/5: Practice financial discipline and continuous learning. Manage expenses wisely, expand financial knowledge, and take control of your financial future. #FinancialDiscipline #LifelongLearning

PROMPT : "Rewrite these tweets in viral form in the style of Linkin Park"

CHATGPT RESPONSE : "1/5: "Unleash the power of financial knowledge, ignite your mind with fire. 'Rich Dad, Poor Dad' lights the path to success, fueling your desire. #MoneyWisdom #LinkinParkInspired

2/5: "Shatter the chains of debt, rise as assets lead the way. 'Rich Dad, Poor Dad' whispers truth, making liabilities fade away. #BreakTheChains #LinkinParkInspired

3/5: "In the realm of abundance, seize opportunities like a fearless warrior. 'Rich Dad, Poor Dad' guides your journey, unlocking treasures hidden in the fire. #AbundanceWarrior #LinkinParkInspired

4/5: "Break free from the race, let financial independence be your salvation. 'Rich Dad, Poor Dad' empowers you to soar, escaping the chains of limitation. #FlyToFreedom #LinkinParkInspired

5/5: "March to the rhythm of discipline, ignite the flames of endless learning. 'Rich Dad, Poor Dad' echoes in your soul, financial mastery forever burning. #DisciplineFlames #LinkinParkInspired"

YOUTUBE VIDEOS

I'm sure you've thought about starting a YouTube channel at least once, and if you already have one, you know how difficult it is to come up with the perfect title, description, and script and more

Normally you'd have to put a lot of effort in...

1.1 Creating an Intriguing Title:
- Use captivating words or questions.
- Accurately represent your video's content.

1.2 Crafting a Compelling Description:
- Summarize content concisely and enticingly.
- Highlight value or benefits for viewers.

2.1 Hooking Your Audience:
- Grab attention with a strong opening.
- Engage with captivating questions or anecdotes.

2.2 Keeping it Concise and Well-Structured:
- Break video into segments for clarity.
- Deliver information in a clear manner.

2.3 Showcasing Expertise and Personality:
- Demonstrate knowledge to establish credibility.
- Infuse unique personality for viewer connection.

2.4 Including a Call to Action:
- End with a clear call to action.
- Encourage likes, comments, subscriptions, or exploration of related content."

Example : Lets say you want to make a video of evolution of human but want the video to be under 4 minutes, we can do something like

PROMPT : Create a youtube video script for a video that is on evolutions of humans but make sure the script length is just enough so everything can be put under a 4 minute video

CHATGPT RESPONSE :
YOUTUBE VIDEO SCRIPT
[Background Music Starts]

[OPENING SHOT: Animated graphics of a timeline unfurling, leading back to prehistoric times]
NARRATOR: (Voiceover) "From swinging in trees to landing on the moon, the story of human evolution is a tale filled with fascinating twists and turns. Today, we're going to take you on a whirlwind journey through millions of years... in just four minutes. Are you ready? Let's dive in!"
[TRANSITION: The screen transitions to an animation of early hominids]
NARRATOR: (Voiceover) "Let's turn the clock back to about 7 million years ago. This is when we

see the first hominids, our earliest ancestors, who split from the lineage that would lead to our closest living relatives: chimpanzees."

[CUT: To an animated early human walking upright]

NARRATOR: (Voiceover) "Fast forward to about 2 million years ago, and we see the rise of Homo erectus, the first of our ancestors to stand upright consistently. They also mastered the use of tools."

[TRANSITION: Screen transitions to a fire being lit]

NARRATOR: (Voiceover) "And what's that glow in the distance? That's right - fire! Homo erectus was likely the first to harness this elemental force, transforming our diet and culture forever"

Well I cut it down here but you know, you can further improve the script by tweaking it a little.

Example : "Lets say you want to create a script for a video for BEST COUNTRY TO LIVE IN THE 21ST Century and it must consider all the factors like GDP, UNEMPLOYMENT AND ON AND THEN PROVIDE YOU WITH THE LIST OF 5-10 such countrys and then you will make a video on it."

PROMPT : Create a script for a video for BEST

COUNTRY TO LIVE IN THE 21ST Century and it must consider all the factors like GDP, UNEMPLOYMENT AND ON AND THEN PROVIDE YOU WITH THE LIST OF 5-10 such country's and then you will make a video on it."

CHATGPT RESPONSE : "[Background music fades in]

Narrator: "Welcome to our channel, where we explore the best countries to live in the 21st century. In this video, we'll delve into various factors such as GDP, unemployment rates, and more, to compile a list of the top 5-10 countries that offer exceptional living standards and opportunities. So, without further ado, let's dive right in!"

[Transition to main content]

[Narrator appears on screen]

Narrator: "When it comes to choosing the best country to live in, there are several critical factors to consider. Let's begin by examining the economic indicators that play a significant role in evaluating a country's potential for a prosperous life."

[Graphics and statistics related to GDP, unemployment rates, and economic growth are shown]

Narrator: "Gross Domestic Product, or GDP, reflects a nation's economic strength and prosperity. High GDP often correlates with better employment opportunities, higher standards of living, and improved infrastructure. Low unemployment rates suggest a stable job market and better chances of finding work."

[Graphics show the top countries based on GDP and low unemployment rates]

Narrator: "Taking these factors into account, here are five countries that excel in economic stability and opportunities:

1. Country A
2. Country B
3. Country C
4. Country D
5. Country E

Did you see how it works, again you can ask it not add add graphics or include some case study and it will do make changes accordingly.

I have also made a YOUTUBE Video so you can have a better understanding , the script was entirely generated by CHATGPT and I just added some stock footages along with AI voice.

If you are reading this on a paperback simply post the url in your browser.

I have shorted the url so its easier for you

1 : https://rb.gy/zi73g

In case it doesn't work .

2:https://www.youtube.com/watchv=buOr254Lsmw

INSTAGRAM REEL

While CHATGPT is useful for making an Instagram reel, you'll have much less time to do so on Instagram. People usually skip reels in under a second, so the hook has to be spot on.

Lets say you want to make a "Day in the Life" video.

PROMPT : "Create a instagram reel script for a day in the life video to end under 45 seconds. Create perfect initial hook and exactly at which frame what do I add with seconds timer"

CHATGPT RESPONSE :

"INSTAGRAM REEL SCRIPT
[FRAME 1 - 0:00-0:02 - Hook] TEXT ON SCREEN: "Ever wondered what a day in my life looks like? Buckle up!"
[Clip: You look into the camera with an excited smile, then transition with a wink or a swipe of hand]

[FRAME 2 - 0:02-0:05] TEXT ON SCREEN: "6:00 AM - Rise and Shine!" [Clip: Alarm clock ringing, you stretching in bed]

[FRAME 3 - 0:05-0:09] TEXT ON SCREEN: "6:30 AM - Fitness first!" [Clip: Quick shots of you doing morning workout/yoga]

[FRAME 4 - 0:09-0:13] TEXT ON SCREEN: "7:30 AM - Power Breakfast!" [Clip: You preparing breakfast, then a shot of a healthy, delicious meal]

[FRAME 5 - 0:13-0:16] TEXT ON SCREEN: "8:00 AM - Work Mode: On!" [Clip: You sitting at your desk, beginning work]

[FRAME 6 - 0:16-0:20] TEXT ON SCREEN: "12:00 PM - Time to refuel"

[Clip: Lunch being served, you enjoying your meal]

[FRAME 7 - 0:20-0:23] TEXT ON SCREEN: "1:00 PM - Back to the grind" [Clip: You working on your computer]

[FRAME 8 - 0:23-0:27] TEXT ON SCREEN: "6:00 PM - Unwind Time" [Clip: You enjoying a hobby, like reading or painting]

[FRAME 9 - 0:27-0:30] TEXT ON SCREEN: "8:00 PM - Dinner & Relax" [Clip: You having dinner, then relaxing on couch with TV]

[FRAME 10 - 0:30-0:34] TEXT ON SCREEN: "10:00 PM - Bedtime Prep" [Clip: You getting ready for bed, brushing teeth]

[FRAME 11 - 0:34-0:37] TEXT ON SCREEN: "11:00 PM - Lights Out!" [Clip: You switching off the light, shot of a dark room]

[FRAME 12 - 0:37-0:40] TEXT ON SCREEN: "And Repeat! That's a wrap!" [Clip: You giving a thumbs up or peace sign]

[FRAME 13 - 0:40-0:45] TEXT ON SCREEN: "Stay tuned for more insights into my life. Like, share and follow!" [Clip: You waving goodbye]

Remember, you need to be super energetic and fast-paced in these shots to keep up with the rhythm of the reel. It's a glimpse into your daily life, so keep it real, keep it fun!"

Well you got the idea , you can from here tweak in more and get it done ever better.

As before you can first ask for an outline and then improve accordingly.

CHAPTER 5 : SOCIAL MEDIA MARKETING

Thriving in the Digital Age, Regardless of Size

Social media marketing is crucial in today's fast-paced, always-evolving world. Whether you're just starting out or have years of experience under your belt, you'll find that marketing is an exciting and challenging field.

Keeping up with the ever-shifting social media algorithms is like a never-ending quest for a hidden treasure. Do what makes the most sense right now, with the understanding that this may change tomorrow. Normally you'll have to :

• Stay up-to-date on what's happening in the world of social media advertising. It's a race that's only getting more intense, and you can't afford to lag behind.

• It's challenging to create engaging content that will resonate with your audience. It must be interesting enough to be talked about and share, and it must also capture the essence of your brand.

- Measuring the ROI of your social media activity can be challenging. The value of Facebook likes, shares, and comments is difficult to quantify.
- Meeting expectations is a skill that requires practice. Their expectations may be too high because of discrepancies between their beliefs and the realities of social media marketing.
- When your team size increases, it can be challenging to keep everyone on the same page. It's like conducting an ensemble of exceptional soloists.
- Successful social media marketing requires a careful balancing act between spontaneity and preparation. Finding the optimal proportions is crucial.
- Trying to get great results while working with a limited budget is similar to walking a tightrope. Making every dollar count is of paramount importance.
- Having to deal with negative comments is just part of life. Even though it can be hard, it's a fact that has to be faced.

Let's say you run a digital marketing business and are always on the lookout for new content ideas for your clients. Here's where your digital partner, ChatGPT, can help. It can help you improve conversions, boost sales for your clients, and, as a result, grow your own business.

Here's how you could swiftly sketch a comprehensive marketing campaign for a variety of social media channels.

Consider a scenario where a client seeks an instant pitch for their new vegan skincare line. They desire a glimpse into the campaign, including probable costs. Here's how ChatGPT could assist:

PROMPT : "Create a pitch for a new vegan skincare line, outlining campaign strategies, target audience, and projected costs."

ChatGPT's Suggestion:

'Embrace the Natural: The Vegan Skincare Revolution'

Target Audience: Health-conscious individuals, aged 20-40 years

Essential Takeaways:
- Step into nature's embrace with our novel vegan skincare line.
- Attuned to the preferences of mindful consumers who value both their skin and the planet.
- Offering the skincare rejuvenation you need, devoid of any animal-derived elements.

- Motto: "Harmony with Nature, Harmony with Your Skin."

Promotion Mediums:
- Social Media (Instagram, Facebook, Pinterest)
- Online avenues (YouTube, lifestyle bloggers)
- Local community events (Farmers markets, Vegan fairs)

Anticipated Expenses:
Social Media Advertising:
- Instagram: $0.50-$2.00 per click, $5-$15 CPM
- Facebook: $0.50-$2.00 per click, $5-$15 CPM
- Pinterest: $0.50-$2.00 per click, $5-$15 CPM

Online platforms:
- YouTube: $0.10-$0.30 per view, $5-$15 CPM
- Bloggers: Depending on influencer's reach and audience engagement, it can vary from $50-$500 per post.
- Local events: Participation costs might range between $100-$500 per event.

Additional Activities:
- Collaborating with popular vegan influencers for product reviews

- Conducting product demonstrations at local farmers markets and vegan festivals
- Launching social media contests and giveaways
- Collaborating with local stores for exclusive in-store promotions and displays."

Example 2 :

Prompt: "ChatGPT, I need to create a marketing strategy for a new line of affordable artificial jewelry aimed at fashion-conscious women aged 18-35. Could you assist me with key messages, selection of promotional channels, cost estimates, and some additional activities to enhance the campaign's reach?"

ChatGPT Response: "Absolutely! Here's a potential strategy:

Campaign Title: 'Revamp Your Style with Allure: The Artificial Jewelry Sensation'

Target Audience: Fashion-forward women, aged 18-35 years

Key Messages:
1. 'Elevate your style quotient with our stunning range of artificial jewelry.'

- 'Experience affordable luxury that brings out your inner diva.'
- 'Redefine fashion, one piece at a time.'
- Slogan: 'Allure: Your Everyday Runway.'

Promotional Channels:

- Social Media: Utilize platforms like Instagram and Pinterest for showcasing your jewelry designs.
- Collaborate with fashion bloggers to reach a wider audience.
- Set up pop-up stores at local fashion events for a real-world presence.

Cost Estimates:

- Social Media Advertising: For platforms like Instagram and Pinterest, you could be looking at about $0.50-$2.00 per click, and $5-$15 CPM.
- Collaboration with fashion bloggers can range from $100-$500 per post, depending on their reach and audience engagement.
- For setting up pop-up stores at local fashion events, rent and setup could be between $200-$800 per event.

You can simply ask CHAGPT to draft a pitch for Twitter and Linkedin by using THIS SAME STYLE to promote on various social media platforms.

I'm using these two as examples, but you can play a lot more.

PROMPT : "For the same product create a Linkedin post acting as a advertising pitch but also keep it professional under 250 words you can also add we re hiring part"

CHATGPT RESPONSE : ***Introducing Allure: Redefining Affordable Luxury in Artificial Jewelry***

Exciting news from our team - we are proud to unveil our innovative Allure collection, a new line of high-quality, affordable artificial jewelry specifically designed for the style-conscious women aged 18-35.

Our mission with Allure is to provide fashionable accessories that enhance everyday style without the luxury price tag. We believe that the key to standing out is not in the cost, but in the uniqueness of design and the quality of craftsmanship.

Under our campaign slogan, "Allure: Your Everyday Runway," we aim to promote the idea that everyone can own their personal style with confidence and grace.

As we embark on this exciting venture, we are also expanding our team and looking for passionate individuals who share our vision. We are currently hiring for several sales roles and invite interested professionals to apply.

Join us in this exciting phase of growth as we redefine affordable luxury in the fashion industry. Reach out for more information on our collection or job opportunities.

#AllureJewelry #RedefiningLuxury #JobOpening #JoinOurTeam #SalesRolesAvailable"

PROMPT : "CREATE A VIRAL STYLE THREAD FOR PROMOTION FOR TWITTER" CREATE 5 TWITTER POSTS, MAKE IT CATCHY , ADD SOME HUMOUR"

1.CHATGPT RESPONSE :

" BREAKING: Unleashing Allure, a fashionable revolution in the artificial jewelry market! Wave goodbye to guilt shopping, we're bringing affordable luxury to the style-conscious women out there. Brace yourself, fashion police! #AllureJewelry #AffordableLuxury #EverydayRunway

2. Picture this: Rocking a unique, high-quality piece of jewelry that makes your wallet smile as much as your mirror reflection. Is this reality or a fashionista's

dream? Spoiler alert: It's both! #AllureJewelry #FashionGoals #NoMoreFashionFauxPas

3. "Allure: Your Everyday Runway" - Because every day deserves a little bit of the red carpet, minus the paparazzi, of course! #RunwayEveryday #AllureJewelry #AffordableGlamour

4. Can't afford to keep up with the Kardashians? Neither can we! But with our new Allure collection, we can sure as heck style like them. Get ready to level up your style game! #AllureJewelry #FashionForward

PSST! Job hunters on Twitter, got an eye for style and a knack for sales? Join the Allure revolution! We're hiring go-getters to help us take over the affordable luxury world. DMs are open for details! #JobOpening #JoinOurTeam #AllureJewelry"

ChatGPT's flexibility allows you to do this again and over again, which opens up even more incredible options.

QUIZ CREATION

Let's now explore the other great features that CHATGPT offers.

Let's imagine you want to check your command of the English language or you're a teacher looking for some free quizzes. Or maybe you wish to evaluate your readiness for the "TECHNICAL ANALYSIS - DERIVATIVES" exam?

You could simply check it with the help of CHATGPT.

Prompt: "Generate a set of 7 multiple-choice questions focused on intermediate English grammar. Each question should provide 4 answer options."

CHATGPT RESPONSE :
"Which of the following sentences is in the past perfect tense?
a) I have eaten sushi before.
b) I ate sushi yesterday.
c) I had eaten sushi before I visited Japan.
d) I will eat sushi tomorrow.

What is the correct plural form of "goose"?
a) Gooses
b) Geese
c) Goosi
d) Goose

What is the correct superlative form of "bad"?
a) Badest
b) Worst
c) Badder
d) Worsest

Which sentence correctly uses a semicolon?
a) I have a big test tomorrow; I can't go to the concert.
b) I have a big test tomorrow, I can't go to the concert.
c) I have a big test tomorrow: I can't go to the concert.
d) I have a big test tomorrow - I can't go to the concert.

What type of verb is "swimming" in this sentence: "I like swimming."
a) Infinitive
b) Gerund
c) Past participle
d) Transitive verb

Which of the following is a passive sentence?
a) The dog chased the cat.
b) The cat was chased by the dog.

c) The cat chased the dog.
d) The dog was chasing the cat.

In the sentence "I gave him a book", what is "a book"?
a) Indirect object
b) Direct object
c) Subject
d) Preposition

"PROMPT" : "PROVIDE ANSWER TO THESE QUESTIONS"

CHATGPT RESPONSE :
- c) I had eaten sushi before I visited Japan.
- b) Geese
- b) Worst
- a) I have a big test tomorrow; I can't go to the concert.
- b) Gerund
- b) The cat was chased by the dog.
- b) Direct object"

We now have all the answer. We could do this for anything, any quiz.
Make sure to recheck answers as CHATGPT may occasionally get it wrong .

NUTRITIONAL DIET

Lets say you want to create a nutrition diet chart for your grandfather who mainly likes to rely on fruits, we could simply.

PROMPT : Create a nutrition guide diet for a 77 year old person who does not each much , make sure to add vegan protein and diet must be 50-60% fruit based, make sure all the food that is added is easy to chew and there must be a gap of atleast 4 hour between each diet and last diet must be at 8:30pm

CHATGPT RESPOMNSE "Here's a nutrition guide diet for a 77-year-old person who doesn't eat much. The diet includes vegan protein sources and is 50-60% fruit-based. All the foods included are easy to chew, and there's a minimum 4-hour gap between each meal. The last meal is to be eaten by 8:30 PM

7:30 AM - Breakfast:
- Smoothie: Blend 1 cup of mixed berries (strawberries, blueberries, raspberries), 1 ripe banana, 1 cup of almond milk, 1 tablespoon of chia seeds, and 1 scoop of vegan protein powder.

Soft oatmeal: Cook 1/2 cup of rolled oats with water until soft.

11:30 AM - Snack:
- Handful of raw almonds or walnuts.
- A small piece of soft fruit like a ripe peach or pear.

3:30 PM - Lunch:
- Chickpea Salad: Mix 1 cup of cooked chickpeas, chopped cucumbers, tomatoes, red onions, and bell peppers. Dress it with a dressing made from lemon juice, olive oil, and herbs.
- Soft steamed vegetables: Steam a variety of soft vegetables such as carrots, zucchini, and broccoli until tender. Season with a sprinkle of salt and pepper.
- Soft whole grain bread: Choose a whole grain bread that is easy to chew. Spread with hummus or avocado.

7:30 PM - Snack:
- Rice cake or whole grain crackers topped with mashed avocado or nut butter.

8:30 PM - Dinner:
- Baked tofu or tempeh: Marinate tofu or tempeh in your favorite vegan sauce and bake until lightly crispy.
- Quinoa and vegetable stir-fry: Sauté mixed vegetables like bell peppers, snap peas.
- Steamed spinach: Steam fresh spinach until wilted and season with a squeeze of lemon juice and a sprinkle of salt."

You could go deeper by asking it to create a 1 month plan for yourself for weight loss or weight gain or more.

PROMPT : "Starting of today , considering it as day one create a 30days plan for me to lose 5kgs , I am 28years old , 6feet and I weight 170 pounds. I want to drop 10 pounds, I am a vegetarian , my only exercise would be 10pushups + 20 minutes of brisk walking, make a plan suitable to me, I can exercise 4 days a week"

CHATGPT RESPONSE :

"Here's a 30-day plan to help you lose 10 pounds (5 kilograms) while considering your vegetarian diet and exercise routine. Though, please note that weight loss varies from person to person"

Day 1-7:
- Diet: Aim for a daily calorie deficit of around 500 calories. Include a variety of plant-based foods in your meals, focusing on whole grains, legumes, vegetables, fruits, and healthy fats.
- Exercise: Perform 10 pushups and engage in brisk walking for 20 minutes four days a week. You can do this routine on alternate days.

Day 8-14:
- Diet: Continue with the calorie deficit and focus on portion control. Incorporate more high-fiber foods to promote satiety and regulate blood sugar levels.
- Exercise: Increase the intensity of your workouts by adding 10 minutes of jogging or running after your brisk walking. Perform the pushups routine on alternate days.

Day 15-21:
- Diet: Keep monitoring your calorie intake and ensure a balanced vegetarian diet. Include protein-rich plant foods such as tofu, tempeh, legumes, and nuts.
- Exercise: Increase the duration of your brisk walking to 30 minutes and maintain the pushups routine on alternate days.

Day 22-28:
- Diet: Continue with the calorie deficit and focus on consuming whole, nutrient-dense foods. Opt for healthy snacks like fruits, nuts, and vegetable sticks.
- Exercise: Add variety to your workouts by incorporating other forms of cardiovascular exercises like cycling or swimming. Perform the pushups routine on alternate days.

Day 29-30:
- Diet: In the last two days, continue with your balanced vegetarian diet and pay attention to portion sizes. Stay consistent with your calorie deficit.
- Exercise: Maintain your exercise routine, ensuring a combination of brisk walking or other cardiovascular exercises along with pushups.

Throughout the 30-day period, it's important to stay hydrated, get adequate sleep, and manage stress levels. Remember, consistency is key. "

COMPLICATED ISSUES

This may seem like a lot to cover, but I want to emphasize what a fantastic time-saving tool ChatGPT can be, particularly for small firms or self-starters. Imagine that you are in charge of a brand-new NGO whose major objective is to assist underprivileged youngsters. Giving them food and knowledge on a regular basis is one of your major tasks. A devoted crew of five volunteers manages everything. You now choose to launch a website in order to expand the NGO's audience.

You are aware that a thorough "Terms and Conditions" section is among the many things it needs, and that this is often something that calls for legal expertise. Here, ChatGPT really shines: This strong AI can make this complicated but necessary piece in seconds, reducing or almost eliminating your need for legal help and letting you focus on what really matters: your goal.

Lets see how we can go by this

PROMPT : "Create full terms and conditions , keeping all the legal aspect in Mind for an NGO based in Minnesota which works for empowerment of children by providing them with mainly education and necessary grocery items"

CHATGPT RESPONSE :
"TERMS AND CONDITIONS

Thank you for visiting and using the website of [NGO Name] ("the Organization"). By accessing and utilizing this website, you agree to comply with and be bound by the following terms and conditions. Please read them carefully.

1. Acceptance of Terms By accessing or using the website, you acknowledge that you have read, understood, and agreed to be bound by these terms and conditions. If you do not agree with any part of these terms, please refrain from using the website.

2. Purpose and Services The Organization is a non-profit entity based in Minnesota that aims to empower underprivileged children by providing education and necessary grocery items. The website serves as a platform to raise awareness, facilitate donations, and provide information about our initiatives.

3. Privacy Policy The Organization respects your privacy and handles personal information in accordance with our Privacy Policy. By using the website, you consent to the collection, use, and disclosure of your personal information as outlined in the Privacy Policy.

4. Intellectual Property All content on the website, including text, graphics, logos, images, audio clips, and software, is the property of the Organization and is protected by intellectual property laws. You may not modify, reproduce, distribute, or create derivative works based on the website content without prior written consent from the Organization.

5. Donations The Organization accepts monetary donations through the website to support its initiatives. All donations are voluntary and non-refundable. The Organization reserves the right to allocate donated funds based on its discretion to further its mission."

Obviously the response by CHATGPT was really big but I cut it down here.

You can definitely alter the prompt of chatgpt for your own need.

CHAPTER 6 : MONETIZING WITH CHATGPT

The New Digital Gold Rush of Passive Income

This is a topic that is extremely close to my heart, and although I have a lot to say, I find it disappointing to see people struggle with knowing precisely where to focus their attention. What you need to realize is that because everyone now has access to CHATGPT, whatever you could accomplish with little effort might be simply duplicated by someone else, putting them on an equal footing with you. So where precisely do we stand to gain? Therefore, the goal is to play the long game.

I want to talk about things that will take you some time to learn. These things won't happen in an instant, but they will help you stay in the game in the long run.

1 : YOUTUBE VIDEOS

We did talk about Youtube initially but lets go deeper now . Personally, I believe that YouTube has been around for a very long time, and I do not anticipate any significant competition for it until at least 2030.

With CHATGPT right there by your side, we can start using YouTube as a terrific passive income source.

For this CHATGPT should be used as an add-on to your ongoing research. To illustrate, let's say you want to start making YouTube videos but are completely unsure of where to begin. Try asking yourself what you enjoy doing instead of worrying about the competition or whether people would even search for it, because billions of people use YouTube, even if only 0.003% of them are marginally interested in what you would like to make videos about. That's a good place to begin with.

EXAMPLE: Lets say you like making pasta and you are really good at it, now we can take help from CHATGPT.

PROMPT : "I want to make pasta video for youtube, I am going to make videos in english , give me some ideas of what can be done"

CHATGPT RESPONSE :

"Classic Italian Pasta Recipes:
- Spaghetti Carbonara
- Fettuccine Alfredo
- Spaghetti Aglio e Olio
- Pasta Primavera
- Linguine with Clam Sauce

1. Regional Pasta Specialties:
   - Lasagna Bolognese (from Bologna, Italy)
   - Penne Arrabbiata (from Rome, Italy)
   - Orecchiette with Broccoli Rabe (from Puglia, Italy)

Pasta alla Norma (from Sicily, Italy)"

Honestly at this point this is not what we are looking . So when CHATGPT does do what we want it to do, we need to tailor our prompt.

PROMPT : "This is going to be my first video , create a complete script and give me a title for the video in viral style and tell me the best pasta to make for the first time so its not complicated for me as a beginner"

CHATGPT RESPONSE :

Title: "Easy-Peasy Creamy Garlic Parmesan Pasta! Creaminess Galore! 😊 "

Introduction: Host (You): "Hey there, pasta lovers! Welcome to my YouTube channel, where we dive into the world of deliciousness! Today, we have something special for all the beginners out there. I'm going to show you how to make a mouthwatering, creamy garlic parmesan pasta that will have you craving for more! It's the perfect dish to kick-start your pasta-making journey. So, let's get cooking!"

Recipe Overview: Host (You): "Our creamy garlic parmesan pasta is a true crowd-pleaser. With a velvety sauce, fragrant garlic, and the richness of parmesan cheese, it's a match made in pasta heaven! Plus, it's super easy to prepare, making it ideal for beginners. Let's take a quick look at the ingredients we'll need."

I like this and based on your liking you can improve further ahead

Lets take another example in this lets assume you just want CHATGPT to do the research work for you from scratch so we can go like.

PROMPT : "Give me youtube video ideas that have a high chance of going viral but also have low competition and a beginner friendly to start with"

CHATGPT RESPONSE :

1. ""10 DIY Room Decor Ideas Under $10 That Will Blow Your Mind!"
2. "5 Quick and Easy Smoothie Recipes for Busy Mornings!"
3. "Photography 101: The Ultimate Beginner's Guide to Stunning Photos!"
4. "Unboxing the Coolest Tech Gadgets of 2023: Review and Reactions!"
5. "10-Minute Beginner's Full-Body Workout: No Equipment Needed!"
6. "Yummy and Healthy Snack Ideas for Kids: Back-to-School Edition!"
7. "Hidden Gems in [Your City]: Must-Visit Spots You Never Knew Existed!"
8. "How to Start a Successful Blog: Step-by-Step Guide for Beginners!"
9. "Mindfulness and Meditation for Stress Relief: Easy Techniques for Beginners!"
10. "Quick and Delicious One-Pot Meals: Perfect for Busy People!"

I think the list is exceptional , either you can choose any of these topics and simply regenerate response.

I personally feel number 3 is an evergreen niche , people would always search on youtube how to click stunning pictures . So lets say we want to go ahead with number 3 , we could go like

PROMPT : "Create a youtube video with exact time frame with a fun script for a video around 5 minutes for number 3"

CHATGPT RESPONSE :

"Title: "Photography 101: The Ultimate Beginner's Guide to Stunning Photos!"

[Opening Scene: Host standing in a picturesque location with a camera in hand]

Host (You): "Hey there, aspiring photographers! Welcome to my channel, where we unlock the secrets of capturing stunning photos. Today, I have something special for all the beginners out there. Get ready to dive into Photography 101, where I'll teach you the fundamentals of taking breathtaking shots. Let's get started!"

[Time Stamp: 0:00 - 0:15]

Scene Transition: Animated camera icon with the title "Understanding Your Camera"

Host (You): "Before we dive into the technicalities, let's start with understanding your camera. Every great photographer needs to know their gear inside out. Don't worry, I'll make it fun and simple!"

[Time Stamp: 0:15 - 1:00]

Host (You): "First things first, let's demystify the exposure triangle. It's the foundation of photography, consisting of aperture, shutter speed, and ISO. Imagine these three elements as a trio of dance partners, working together to create the perfect exposure!"

[Time Stamp: 1:00 - 1:45]

Scene Transition: Host demonstrating with props to represent aperture, shutter speed, and ISO

Host (You): "Aperture is like a pair of sunglasses for your camera lens, controlling the amount of light entering. Shutter speed is the gatekeeper of time, determining how long the sensor is exposed. And ISO? It's the camera's sensitivity to light, like an amplifier for low-light situations!"

Although I cut it down, you still got the idea. Of course, if you know a lot about photography-related topics, it could be a wonderful idea, but you can choose a different topic in the same way if you don't.

It takes time, and you won't suddenly have a video go viral with a million views in a day, but everything will eventually fall into place.

PART II: *There are two ways to create YouTube videos: one without displaying your face, the other with it.*

If it's the second part, then nothing more needs to be said; just experiment and you'll figure it out. However, if you don't want to reveal your face, you can use a tool called Pictory, which will create stock footage for you based on the text and even has an AI voice character built in.

Additional Advice: The success of your content depends on how well your thumbnail performs. If the thumbnail doesn't grab viewers' attention, even the best video you've ever made might not be seen. Consider drawing ideas from channels like MrBeast, known for its appealing thumbnails.

(A YouTube thumbnail is a brief, appealing image that serves as a video's representation and persuades users to click and watch.)

BOOKS / EBOOKS

With the help of CHATGPT, it's become a lot easier to publish an ebook or book. But this presents a problem: in a world where anyone can write, how do you make your work stand out? Royalties are a great way to make money over the long run. When you choose to publish on AMAZON.COM, you don't have to worry about trying to find a publisher as it does all the work for you. Just the work must be interesting and meet Amazon's quality standards. Even though you, as the author, write the content, Amazon's image is at stake, so they want to make sure that only high-quality work is displayed on their website.

We will talk about ebook primarily but the way to make them for both is the same.

A good e-book can indeed be a demanding endeavor, requiring careful attention to multiple aspects. Here are eleven key considerations that must be taken care of:

1. "Define your goal: Clarify your purpose for writing the ebook.

2. Identify your target audience: Determine who your ebook is intended for.
3. Conduct market research: Explore existing ebooks in your niche.
4. Outline your content: Create a clear outline or structure for your ebook.
5. Set a realistic timeline: Establish a reasonable timeline for completing your ebook.
6. Research and gather information: Conduct thorough research on your chosen topic.
7. Develop a captivating title: Craft a compelling title that grabs attention.
8. Create engaging and concise content: Write in a clear and concise manner.
9. Edit and proofread meticulously: Review your content for clarity and accuracy.
10. Design an eye-catching cover: Create a visually appealing cover that reflects your ebook's essence.
11 : Plan your ebook's distribution: Determine how you will distribute and market your ebook"

Again with CHATGPT almost 80% of the things will automatically be taken care of?
As we did with youtube video we will take the same example so its simpler to understand.

PROMPT : ""Provide me with an outline for an ebook to be written on Photography tips 101"

CHATGPT RESPONSE
: "Title: Photography Tips 101: Capturing Stunning Images with Confidence

Introduction:
- The importance of photography and the power of visual storytelling
- Setting the stage for learning essential photography tips and techniques

Chapter 1: Understanding Your Camera
- Exploring the different types of cameras and their features
- Mastering the settings: aperture, shutter speed, ISO, and white balance
- Navigating through camera modes for various shooting situations

Chapter 2: Composition Techniques for Impactful Photos
- The rule of thirds and other compositional guidelines
- Balancing elements and creating visual interest
- Using lines, shapes, and patterns to enhance your images

Chapter 3: Mastering Lighting and Exposure

- Harnessing natural light: golden hour, blue hour, and diffused light
- Using artificial lighting techniques for indoor and low-light conditions
- Understanding exposure and achieving the right balance

Chapter 4: Capturing Dynamic Landscapes and Stunning Nature

- Landscape photography essentials: finding compelling locations and viewpoints
- Working with foreground, midground, and background elements

Again I cut it but that's how we get started. The advantage we can in ebook over youtube video for this specific topic is , in a youtube video you might need a camera and would have to physically explain every aspect .

When writing an ebook, you have the freedom to go into great detail and supplement your explanation with a variety of images to aid in comprehension. This proves advantageous for individuals who prefer not to venture into creating a YouTube video on the topic.

Now let's assign another task to CHATGPT and wait in anticipation of the results that it will produce for us.

PROMPT : Provide some ebook ideas that are often avoided or have low competition but reasonable demand

CHATGPT RESPONSE :

"Here are some ebook title ideas with low competition but reasonable demand:

1. "Thrifty Travel Secrets: Discovering Affordable Adventures"
2. "Small Space Gardening: Green Solutions for Urban Living"
3. "Mindful Eating: Nourishing Body and Soul"
4. "Holistic Wellness for Busy Professionals"
5. "Digital Detox: Reconnecting with Reality"
6. "Introduction to Minimalism: Embracing Simplicity"
7. "Healthy Snacks on the Go: Fueling Your Busy Lifestyle"
8. "Financial Freedom for Millennials: Building Wealth with Confidence"
9. "Unleash Your Passion: Unlocking Creative Potential"

10. "The Art of Journaling: A Path to Self-Discovery"

To enhance the quality of an ebook, it can indeed be beneficial to focus on a niche within a niche or a sub-niche rather than tackling a broad topic. By narrowing down the subject matter, you can provide more in-depth information and cater to a specific audience, making your ebook more valuable and engaging.

For this we can use ,

PROMPT " Give me 3 ideas for a niche that has multiple niches within it "

CHATGPT RESPONSE :

1 : Small Space Gardening: Green Solutions for Urban Living"

- This title can cover various sub-niches such as balcony gardening, rooftop gardening, indoor gardening, vertical gardening, and container gardening. Each sub-niche can have its own chapter or section in the book.

1. "Holistic Wellness for Busy Professionals"

- This title can encompass sub-niches such as stress management techniques, time-efficient workouts, mindfulness practices,

- healthy eating habits for a busy lifestyle, and work-life balance strategies. Each sub-niche can be explored in dedicated chapters or sections.
- "Financial Freedom for Millennials: Building Wealth with Confidence"
  - This title can cover sub-niches such as budgeting and saving strategies, investing for millennials, managing student loans, starting a side hustle, and long-term financial planning. Each sub-niche can be addressed in specific chapters or sections of the book."

I think this is where its best to get started.
 Lets create an outline for indoor gardening. From " Small Space Gardening: Green Solutions for Urban Living"
PROMPT : "Create an outline for indoor gardening"

CHATGPT RESPONSE :
 "Title: Indoor Gardening: Cultivating Green Spaces in Your Home
Introduction:

- The benefits of indoor gardening and its growing popularity
- Setting the stage for creating an indoor garden oasis

Chapter 1: Getting Started with Indoor Gardening

- The basics of indoor gardening: benefits, considerations, and challenges
- Selecting the right indoor plants for your space and lifestyle
- Understanding lighting requirements and optimizing natural and artificial light sources

Chapter 2: Setting Up Your Indoor Garden

- Choosing suitable containers and potting mix for indoor plants
- Creating a conducive environment: temperature, humidity, and ventilation
- Arranging your indoor garden for aesthetic appeal and optimal plant growth

Chapter 3: Nurturing Your Indoor Plants

- Watering techniques: understanding moisture needs and avoiding overwatering
- Fertilizing indoor plants for optimal growth and health

- Pruning, trimming, and supporting indoor plants for proper maintenance

Chapter 4: Dealing with Common Indoor Gardening Challenges

- Identifying and preventing common pests and diseases in indoor plants
- Managing humidity levels and preventing mold or fungal growth
- Troubleshooting plant-specific issues and providing remedies

Chapter 5: Indoor Gardening Techniques and Design Ideas

- Exploring various indoor gardening techniques: hydroponics, vertical gardening, and terrariums
- Creating themed indoor gardens: herb gardens, succulent displays, and air-purifying plant arrangements
- Incorporating creative design elements: decorative containers, trellises, and plant stands

Chapter 6: Enhancing Your Indoor Garden Experience

DIY projects for indoor gardening: creating a self-watering system, propagating plants, and making natural fertilizers

- Using indoor plants for air purification and improving indoor air quality
- Mindful practices: connecting with nature and finding relaxation through indoor gardening

Conclusion:
- Reflecting on the joys and benefits of indoor gardening
- Encouragement to continue exploring and expanding your indoor garden

Additional resources for further guidance and inspiration"

I believe this outline to be remarkable, but if you have any concerns that the ebook's six chapters are simply too few, you can simply write a new prompt asking it to add up to twelve chapters, at which point it will generate a new outline, and you can then ask CHATGPT to elaborate on each topic.

Lets expand on CHAPTER 1

"PROMPT : : For chapter 1 write upto 120 words"
(I implied that it be kept to 120 words, but you may use up to 2000 words.) I've noticed that CHATGPT frequently starts repeating itself when you ask it to build things big in one go, so going beyond 2000 words might not be a good idea.

- CHATGPT RESPONSE :
- "Chapter 1: The Basics of Indoor Gardening: Benefits, Considerations, and Challenges
- Indoor gardening offers a myriad of benefits, bringing nature's beauty and the joy of gardening into the comfort of your home. Discover the advantages of indoor gardening, including improved air quality, stress reduction, and the ability to grow plants year-round.
- However, there are essential considerations to keep in mind. Factors such as available space, lighting conditions, and plant selection play a crucial role in successful indoor gardening. Understanding the unique challenges of indoor environments, such as humidity control and pest management, is vital for maintaining healthy plants.
- In this chapter, we delve into the benefits of indoor gardening, discuss important considerations for setting up your indoor garden, and address the challenges that may arise. By grasping these fundamentals, you'll be well-prepared to embark on your indoor gardening journey with confidence.

- Now that we are done with the main point , we need a title a subtitle (optional) and a description.

PROMPT : "CREATE 10 titles for this ebook"

1. CHATGPT RESPONSE : "Indoor Gardening: Cultivating Nature's Beauty within Your Home"
2. "The Joy of Indoor Gardens: Bringing Nature Indoors"
3. "Greening Your Space: A Guide to Successful Indoor Gardening"
4. "Thriving Inside: Secrets to Successful Indoor Plant Care"
5. "Indoor Gardening 101: Growing Plants with Confidence"
6. "Transform Your Home with Indoor Gardens: Tips and Techniques"
7. "Indoor Oasis: Creating a Serene and Vibrant Indoor Garden"
8. "The Art of Indoor Gardening: Nurturing Nature at Home"
9. "From Seed to Splendor: Mastering Indoor Plant Cultivation"
10. "Indoor Gardening Essentials: Techniques for a Flourishing Indoor Garden"

- I personally feel number 3 is the best here but you can choose any title that suits your liking and how you end up altering you book.

Lets create a description now .

PROMPT : "Create a fascinating description for this ebook"

CHATGPT : "Description: "Indoor Gardening: Cultivating Nature's Beauty within Your Home"
Transform your living space into a lush oasis with "Indoor Gardening: Cultivating Nature's Beauty within Your Home." This comprehensive ebook is your guide to the world of indoor gardening, allowing you to bring the wonders of nature indoors and create a serene and vibrant environment.

Discover the joys and benefits of indoor gardening as you learn how to nurture a variety of plants within the comfort of your own home. From choosing the perfect indoor plants to understanding their specific care requirements, this ebook provides you with the essential knowledge and techniques to cultivate thriving green spaces.

Navigate through the considerations unique to indoor gardening, such as optimizing lighting conditions, managing humidity levels, and troubleshooting common challenges. Uncover the secrets to successful plant care, from watering techniques to fertilization, and gain insights into creative design ideas that will enhance the aesthetics of your indoor garden.

Whether you're a novice or experienced gardener, "Indoor Gardening: Cultivating Nature's Beauty within Your Home" equips you with the tools and confidence to embark on your indoor gardening journey. Embrace the tranquility and beauty of nature within your living space and create an indoor oasis that will delight your senses and uplift your spirits."

I think the progress we've made so far is fantastic. If you recall from earlier chapters, we can also use those skills to promote the book.

Lets do it in 2 ways by creating a viral tweet and by writing an outline for Instagram ads so we could promote this book.

PROMPT : 'For this book I have chosen the title "Greening Your Space: A Guide to Successful Indoor Gardening, Create a viral tweet in a funny style"
"

"Tweet 1: Ready to turn your home into a tropical paradise? Get your green thumb ready because "Greening Your Space: A Guide to Successful Indoor Gardening" is here to help!
Say goodbye to boring beige walls and hello to lush greenery! Let's transform our spaces into an indoor jungle and embrace our inner plant whisperers! #GreeningYourSpace #IndoorGardening #PlantWhisperer

Tweet 2: Tired of your plants ghosting you? "Greening Your Space: A Guide to Successful Indoor Gardening" has got you covered! Learn the secret language of plants and finally understand what they're trying to tell you. No more guessing games! Get ready for deep conversations with your leafy friends!

#GreeningYourSpace #PlantCommunication #LeafyConversations

Tweet 3: Who needs a therapist when you can have plants as your listening buddies? Dive into "Greening Your Space: A Guide to Successful Indoor Gardening" and discover the therapeutic benefits of nurturing indoor plants. They're great listeners, non-judgmental, and always there to brighten up your day! ☺ #GreeningYourSpace #PlantTherapy #ListeningBuddies

Tweet 4: Tired of boring home workouts? ♂ Spice things up with "Greening Your Space: A Guide to Successful Indoor Gardening"! Get fit and flex those gardening muscles as you prune, water, and care for your indoor plants. It's a workout that nourishes your soul and keeps your plants thriving! ♀ #GreeningYourSpace #GardeningWorkout #FitAndLeafy

Tweet 5: Calling all aspiring plant chefs! Unleash your culinary creativity with "Greening Your Space: A Guide to Successful Indoor Gardening"! Grow your own herbs, spices, and edible plants right in your kitchen!

Cook with homegrown flavors and take your dishes to the next level! Bon appétit!
#GreeningYourSpace #PlantChefs #HomegrownFlavors

I am once again in awe of CHATGPT's efforts and feel compelled to start gardening for myself. LOL.

Now Lets now move to running Instagram Ads:

PROMPT : "Create an outline for Instagram ads tell me the exact target , age , amount to get started . I want to primarily target people living in the United States"

CHATGPT RESPONSE :

"Instagram Ad Campaign: Indoor Gardening Made Easy

Target Audience:
- Location: United States
- Age: 25-45
- Interests: Gardening, Home Decor, DIY Projects, Sustainable Living, Wellness

Ad 1:

- Visual: A beautifully decorated indoor garden with vibrant plants, cozy seating, and natural light.
- Caption: "Discover the joys of indoor gardening! Transform your home into a green oasis with our expert tips and techniques. Get started today! #IndoorGardeningMadeEasy"

Ad 2:

- Visual: A before-and-after image of a dull space transformed into a lush indoor garden.
- Caption: "Tired of dull spaces? Spruce up your home with indoor gardening! Learn how to choose the perfect plants, create stunning arrangements, and breathe life into your living space. #IndoorGardeningMadeEasy"

Ad 3:

- Visual: A close-up shot of a person happily tending to their indoor plants.
- Caption: "Discover the therapeutic benefits of indoor gardening! It's not just about plants; it's about finding peace and connecting with nature in the comfort of your home. Start your indoor gardening journey today! #IndoorGardeningMadeEasy"

Ad Budget:
- Recommended starting budget: $20-40$ per day
- Monitor the performance of the ads and adjust the budget accordingly to maximize reach and engagement.

By targeting the specific audience parameters and crafting compelling visuals and captions, this Instagram ad campaign aims to capture the attention of individuals living in the United States who are interested in gardening, home decor, and sustainable living

BLOG POSTS

Now that we've covered the basics of brainstorming and how it works, let's delve into more advanced strategies. With a clear understanding of how CHATGPT operates, we can explore ways to create blogs that enable you to earn independently, rather than relying solely on advertisements displayed when visitors access your blog.

Suppose you aspire to write a blog while also venturing into consulting or coaching. In such a scenario, we could consider a approach like the following:

PROMPT: "Give me 5 blog post ideas which I can eventually tap people into converting for coaching "

CHATGPT RESPONSE :
1 : "The Ultimate Guide to [Your Niche]: Unleashing Your Full Potential"
- In this comprehensive guide, provide valuable insights, tips, and strategies that showcase your expertise in your niche. Demonstrate your ability to help readers achieve their goals and highlight the benefits of working with a coach or

consultant to maximize their success.

2 : "Breaking Through Barriers: Overcoming [Specific Challenge] and Thriving"

- Identify a common challenge or obstacle within your niche and offer practical advice, techniques, and personal anecdotes on how to overcome it. Highlight the transformation and growth that can be achieved with the guidance and support of a coach or consultant.

3 : "Mastering Self-Confidence: Unlocking Your Full Potential"

- Explore the concept of self-confidence and its impact on personal and professional success within your niche. Share practical tips, exercises, and mindset shifts to help readers boost their confidence and showcase how working with a coach or consultant can accelerate their confidence-building journey.

4 : "Navigating Career Transitions: Discovering Your True Passion and Finding Fulfillment"

- Address the challenges and uncertainties associated with career transitions, offering guidance and strategies for individuals seeking a more fulfilling professional path within your niche. Highlight the value of working with a coach or consultant to navigate these transitions, clarify goals, and develop a roadmap for success.

5 : "Unlocking Sustainable Weight Loss: Building Healthy Habits for Life"

Provide insights, evidence-based strategies, and practical tips for sustainable weight loss within your niche. Discuss the importance of mindset, nutrition, exercise, and habit formation, emphasizing the benefits of working with a coach or consultant to support and guide individuals on their weight loss journey

So you know where we're going from here, since we can get people to not only see our ads but also get them advice and coaching, which will increase our income.

- Lets go ahead with Number 5 : that is
- "Unlocking Sustainable Weight Loss: Building Healthy Habits for Life"

PROMPT :

"Give title ideas for number 5 in a way that in the end I can provide women over the age of 40 with a personalized diet plan to lose weight"

CHATGPT RESPONSE :
- ""Shaping Your Journey: A Customized Diet Plan for Women Over 40"
- "Age-Defying Weight Loss: Tailored Diet Solutions for Women 40+"
- "Slim & Thriving at 40+: Your Personalized Diet Roadmap"
- "Unlocking Lasting Weight Loss: Nourishing Your Body After 40"
- "Revitalize & Shed Pounds: A Personalized Diet Plan for Women 40+"
- "Diet Secrets for Ageless Wellness: Women's Weight Loss 40+"
- "Transforming Your Health: A Personalized Diet Guide for Women Over 40"
- "Blasting Through Weight Loss Plateaus: Customized Diet Tips for 40+ Women"
- "Elevate Your Fitness: Personalized Diet Strategies for Women 40 and Beyond"
- "40 and Fabulous: Your Custom Diet Plan for Effortless Weight Loss"

Lets go ahead with the sixth one and see what we get from here

PROMPT : " PROVIDE A OUTLINE FOR TITLE 6 "

CHATGPT RESPONSE

: "Title: "Diet Secrets for Ageless Wellness: Women's Weight Loss 40+"

Introduction:

- Highlight the unique challenges women face with weight loss and wellness as they age.
- Emphasize the importance of a personalized diet plan for achieving sustainable weight loss and overall well-being.

Chapter 1: Understanding the Changing Needs of Women's Bodies

- Discuss the hormonal changes and metabolic shifts that occur with age.
- Explain how these changes impact weight loss and the importance of adapting dietary strategies accordingly.

Chapter 2: Nourishing Your Body with Age-Defying Foods

- Highlight nutrient-rich foods that support weight loss and overall health for women over 40.

Provide guidance on portion control, balanced meal planning, and mindful eating practices."

I've shortened it here. As you know, our ultimate goal was to get into consulting or coaching.

Which brings us to our next chapter that is :

COURSE CREATION

Now we have to make a personalized diet plan that explains why and how our diet is important, especially for women over 40, and add all the relevant information to our course.

We would need a plan because we already know what the course will be about.

"Women over 40 wanting to be fit , lose weight and look young again"

PROMPT :

" I am planning to create a course for this blog I have written for women over 40 to lose weight and look and feel young again . Follow absolute logical sequence without repeating or overlapping context and create a proper structure outline for my course "

CHATGPT RESPONSE :

"Course Outline: Ageless Wellness - The Complete Guide to Weight Loss and Rejuvenation for Women Over 40

Module 1: Introduction to Ageless Wellness

- Understanding the unique challenges women over 40 face in achieving weight loss and rejuvenation goals
- Setting realistic expectations and defining the vision for ageless wellness
- Exploring the mind-body connection and its impact on overall well-being

Module 2: Assessing Your Current State

- Conducting a comprehensive self-assessment of health, lifestyle, and weight loss goals
- Identifying personal barriers and challenges that may hinder progress
- Setting measurable and achievable targets for weight loss and rejuvenation

Module 3: Nourishing Your Body for Ageless Wellness

- Understanding the nutritional needs of women over 40 for weight loss and vitality
- Designing a balanced and personalized meal plan to support weight loss and overall well-being
- Incorporating anti-aging foods, superfoods, and targeted supplements for optimal results

Module 4: Exercise and Fitness for Ageless Wellness

- Customizing a fitness regimen to support weight loss, strength, and energy

- Incorporating cardio, strength training, and flexibility exercises into a sustainable fitness routine
- Exploring alternative fitness practices that promote rejuvenation and enhance well-being

Module 5: Unlocking the Power of Hormones and Metabolism

- Understanding the role of hormones and metabolism in weight loss and age management
- Strategies for balancing hormones and optimizing metabolic function through nutrition and lifestyle choices

Addressing common hormone-related challenges and incorporating solutions for long-term success"

Isn't it amazing? We now have a complete course ready to go! You can use your own voice and style for each topic, or easily incorporate stock footage using Pictory. Once your content is prepared, you can simply host it on platforms like Skillshare. Remember, the pricing can vary significantly, so it's a good idea to check out competitors on Skillshare to see how they price their courses based on the subject's complexity and length.

CHAPTER 7 : MAKE IT BIG WITH FREELANCING

The freelance opportunity for those who can utilize CHATGPT effectively has never been this promising. It provides an unmatched advantage to freelancers who can harness its capabilities while also offering a customized structure and tailored solutions to clients. While CHATGPT may generate complex language, it's crucial for you to translate the data into easy-to-understand content. Websites like Quillbot can assist in simplifying the language.

Now, let's dive into the topic of freelance services. There are numerous websites where you can offer your skills and get paid anywhere from $5 to $5000, depending on the complexity of the work. Platforms like Upwork and Fiverr are popular choices, and we'll focus on Fiverr here.

Here are a few insider tips that are often overlooked in most books on this subject. People who are busy writing often forget to share their own experiences and advice on effectively utilizing the Fiverr site.

If you're new to the platform, there are specific rules for setting up your Fiverr account. You can create a maximum of 7 "gigs" from a wide range of over 300 different services. This quota should be taken seriously. When choosing your services, consider your skills and interests to ensure you offer only the best solutions to clients.

A "gig" on Fiverr is a service you offer to potential clients that you will do a certain job. These gigs cover a wide range of tasks, from writing an interesting blog post to giving a brand a unique image. As the person who makes a gig, you get to set your own prices and decide how long it will take you to do the job. Then, potential buyers can look through your gigs and choose the ones that meet their needs and standards.

Some examples of gigs that you can offer on Fiverr:
- Writing and editing
- Graphic design
- Social media marketing
- Virtual assistance

These are some categories , once you visit the website you will find over 300 categories and multiple sub niches in each.
Writing and editing itself has multiple sub-niches.

Lets start with blog post.

You obviously know how to write a blog post with CHATGPT. Now lets go through fiverr on how people are offering their services.

BLOG POSTS

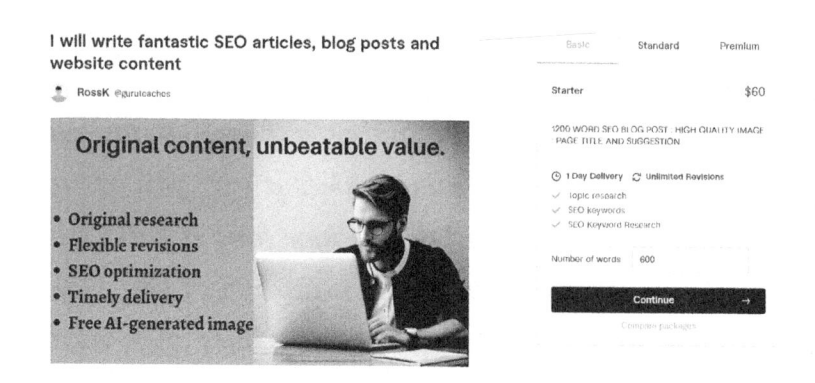

Take a look at this individual charging $60 for a 1200-word blog post with a 1-day delivery time. While you have the freedom to set your own delivery time, I recommend keeping it within a maximum of 2 days. Based on my experience, if you can consistently deliver high-quality work within 2 days, Fiverr tends to rank you higher in search results. However, always prioritize the quality of your work above all else.

AD - COPY

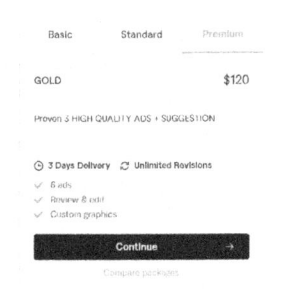

This professional specializes in crafting compelling ad copies, which we've already discussed in our previous conversation. Ad copies encompass the description and pitch of a product or service, and they can be effortlessly generated using CHATGPT. This individual charges approximately $120 for 3 high-quality ads, along with incorporating client input to further enhance the results. You can utilize similar descriptions to attract a broader range of clients and showcase your ability to deliver impactful ad copies.

TRANSLATION SERVICE

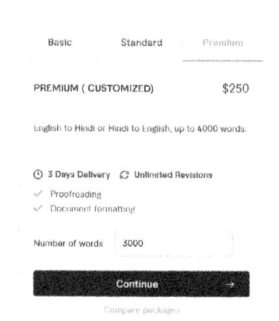

This gentleman specializes in translation services and charges $250 for translating a text of approximately 4000 words. While CHATGPT can be used for assistance, it may not be as proficient in local languages. In such cases, manual restructuring of words and sentences may be necessary. However, considering the compensation of $250 for this job, it's a reasonable rate.

GHOST WRITING

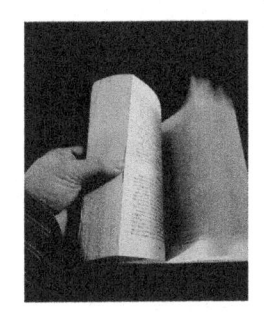

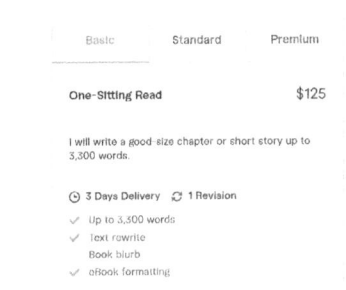

	Basic	Standard	Premium
One-Sitting Read			$125

I will write a good-size chapter or short story up to 3,300 words.

- 🕒 3 Days Delivery   🔄 1 Revision
- ✓ Up to 3,300 words
- ✓ Text rewrite
- Book blurb
- ✓ eBook formatting

By definition : A ghostwriter is a writer who writes a book, article, or other piece of work for someone else, who is then credited as the author. The ghostwriter's name is not revealed to the public. Ghostwriters are often used by celebrities, politicians, and other public figures who want to write a book but don't have the time or the writing skills to do it themselves.

With the help of CHATGPT, it's much faster to write a 3300-word short story.

This man charges $125 for a story like this, and you can finish it in a couple of hours with CHATGPT. Since CHATGPT works quickly, you can make short stories that are interesting in a short amount of time.

As you explore Fiverr, you'll discover various services offered by different freelancers. It's not uncommon to find people charging very high prices, like $5000, for seemingly simpler tasks. Although these tasks may appear straightforward, it's important to understand that these freelancers have built a strong reputation over many years.

When you start on Fiverr, it's a good idea to set reasonable prices and focus on delivering excellent work to your clients. By providing great value and consistently receiving positive reviews, you'll gain credibility and trust within the Fiverr community. Over time, as you receive more positive feedback and establish yourself as a reliable and talented freelancer, the Fiverr algorithm will recognize your reputation and rank you higher in search results.

Once you have a solid foundation of positive reviews, you can gradually increase your prices to reflect your value and expertise. Clients will be willing to pay more for your services, knowing that they can rely on your track record of delivering exceptional results.

Remember, building a successful freelance career on Fiverr takes time, dedication, and a focus on consistently delivering high-quality work. By starting with reasonable pricing and building your reputation, you'll pave the way for long-term success and the ability to charge premium rates for your exceptional services.

ADDITIONAL TIP TO KEEP IN MIND WHEN USING FIVERR:

Once you create your account and activate your gigs, you may receive numerous messages from individuals asking you to connect with them on external platforms like Telegram. It's important to be cautious because interacting or transacting outside of Fiverr is not allowed and goes against the platform's policies. These messages often come from scammers or individuals trying to bypass Fiverr's system.

To protect yourself and maintain a strong reputation on Fiverr, it is mandatory to avoid any transactions or interactions outside of the platform. This means that all communication, project details, and payments should be conducted solely through Fiverr. By adhering to this rule, you ensure a secure and trustworthy environment for both you and your clients.

Remember, by following Fiverr's guidelines and conducting all business within the platform, you safeguard yourself from potential risks and maintain the integrity of your reputation on Fiverr.

CHAPTER 8 : LIMITATIONS

ChatGPT is an excellent tool, but it doesn't know everything. Its understanding of the real world is shaped by the data it was taught on, and as of September 2021, its facts remain static and won't change. It might not always have the most up-to-date knowledge or know what's going on in the world. But since GPT-4 came out, it can now browse data, which is a tool that is still being worked on. As this tool keeps getting better, we can look forward to an AI helper that is smarter and knows more.

Inability to Reason: ChatGPT can give answers, but it doesn't understand why those answers are valid. It gives answers based on patterns it has learned from training data. This can lead to replies that are wrong or don't make sense.

Sensitivity to Input Wording: How you ask a question or give a suggestion can have a big effect on how ChatGPT answers. Small changes in how you word your questions can lead to different answers, so it's important to be clear and detailed.

A tendency to give answers that sound plausible but aren't true: ChatGPT can sometimes give answers that sound plausible but aren't true. Before relying on information, it's important to check the facts and make sure it comes from trusted sources.

ChatGPT learns from the data it is taught on, which can include biased or offensive content found on the internet. It's important to be careful and skeptical about the answers it gives.

Responses That Can't Be Predicted or Aren't Appropriate: Because ChatGPT is trained on internet data, it can sometimes give answers that can't be predicted or aren't appropriate. It's important to use the tool in a responsible way and let people know about any bad results.

Can't Understand humor: ChatGPT has trouble understanding humor or language with nuances. It might take sarcastic comments literally, which could lead to misunderstandings or answers that don't make sense. It's important to avoid sarcasm when talking to ChatGPT so that conversations are correct and useful.

Despite these limitations, ChatGPT shows itself to be a very useful tool for many tasks, as it can handle many questions and assignments with ease. It isn't perfect or all-knowing, like most things in life, but it does an exceptional job of assisting people. Even though we can't count on ChatGPT for everything, it's important to remember that it's a good partner for most things and has consistently shown its worth in the field of AI technology.

CONCLUSION

To sum up, the wise use of ChatGPT offers enormous potential for professional achievement, financial gain, and the acceleration of society growth. With the right direction, this super-technology can produce results that would take years for humans to do on their own. It has a wide range of talents, including writing screenplays, creating YouTube video, creating podcasts, and creating channels for long-term passive income. However, it's vital to keep in mind that ChatGPT is not perfect and can occasionally deliver unexpected or inaccurate results. Recognizing this encourages a cautious and responsible use of technology.

Consider ChatGPT your coach as you go on an exciting road to financial independence. Always keep in mind that building wealth is a marathon, not a sprint; patience, consistency, and steady measures can help you reach your financial objectives. Keep in mind that as you use ChatGPT to your advantage, your success adds to the overall trajectory of human achievement.

We are on the edge of an exciting new age where the fusion of human potential and AI leads to unanticipated opportunities by harnessing the power of this super-technology. Together, let's take this step, utilizing ChatGPT for the common good while simultaneously paving our paths to prosperity.

THANK-YOU NOTE

Dear Reader,

Thank you for reading this book! I genuinely hope you enjoyed it and gained valuable knowledge from its pages. Remember, learning is an ongoing process that should never cease.

If you found this book to be impactful and insightful, I would like to wholeheartedly request your support by leaving a review. Your feedback is incredibly valuable to me, as it not only helps me improve as an author but also enables other readers to discover and benefit from this book.

Your review will play a crucial role in shaping my future work and assisting fellow individuals in making an informed decision about whether this book is right for them. Your honest thoughts will provide invaluable guidance.

Once again, thank you for your time and for being a part of this journey. Your support means the world to me.

Made in United States
Orlando, FL
29 June 2023